Tracing and writing number 1 to 5.

	1	1	1	1	1
	2	2	2	2	2
	3	3	3	3	3
	4	4	4	4	4
	5	5	5	5	5

Tracing and writing number 6 to 10.

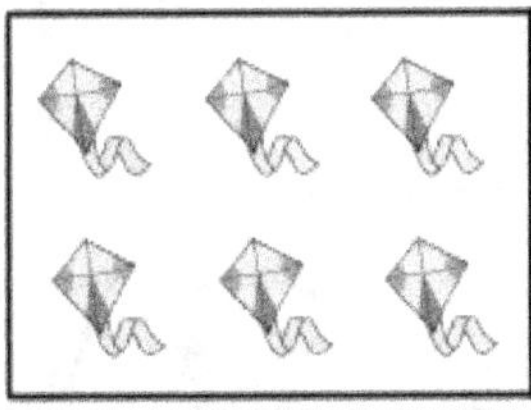	6	6	6	6	6
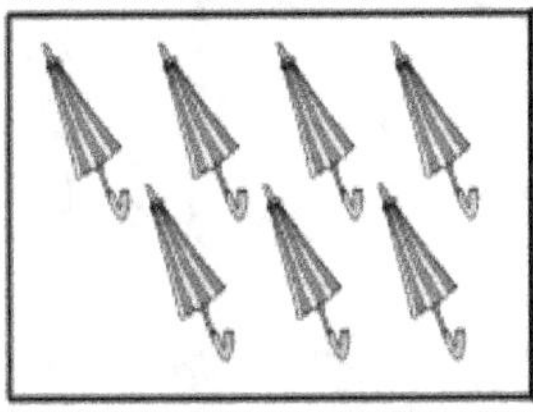	7	7	7	7	7
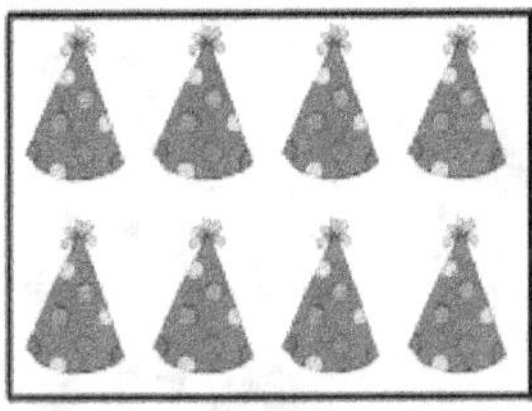	8	8	8	8	8
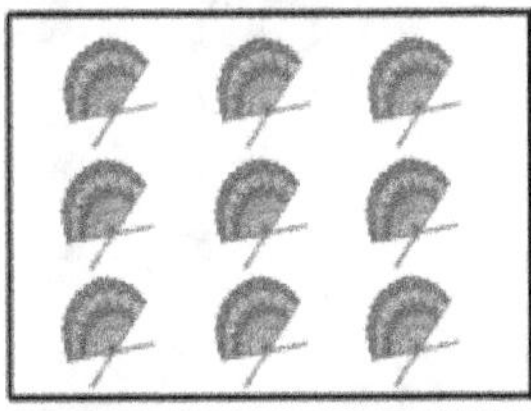	9	9	9	9	9
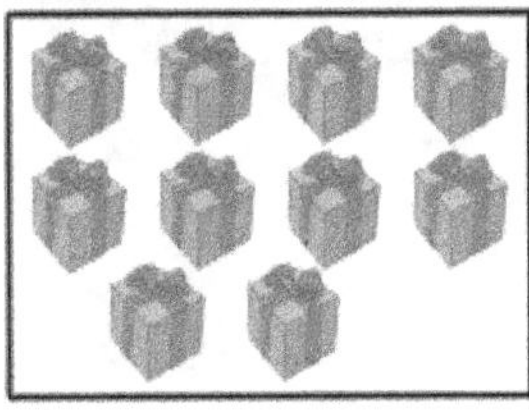	10	10	10	10	10

Counting

How many?

Counting practice up to 10.

Count and write the correct number in the box.

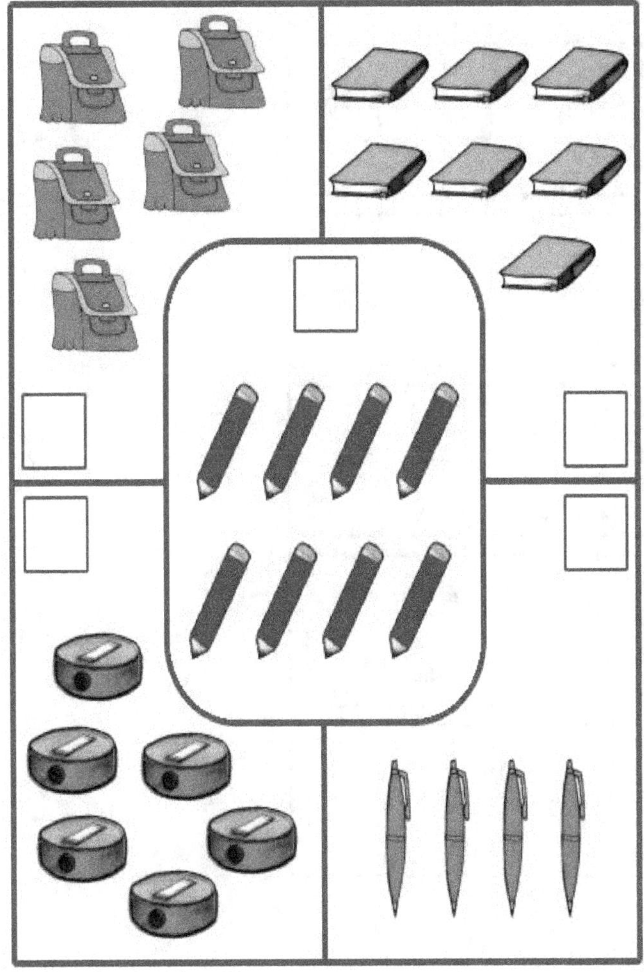

Count and then draw line to the correct numbers.

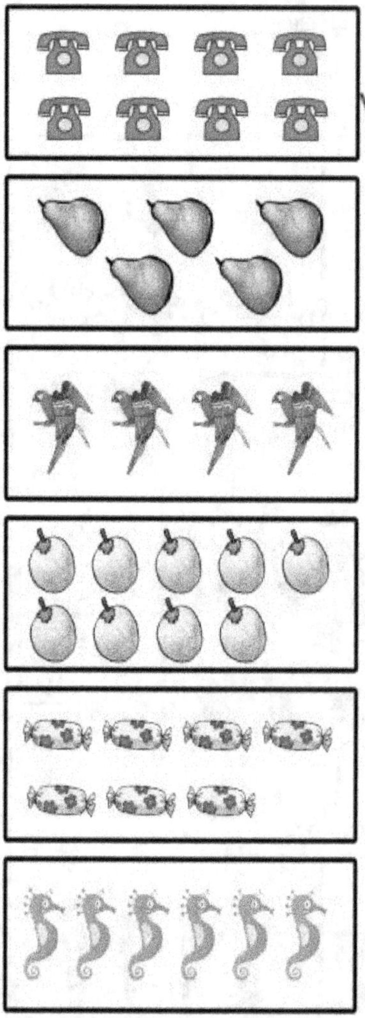

4

5

6

7

8

9

Counting practice up to 10.

Count and write the correct number in the box.

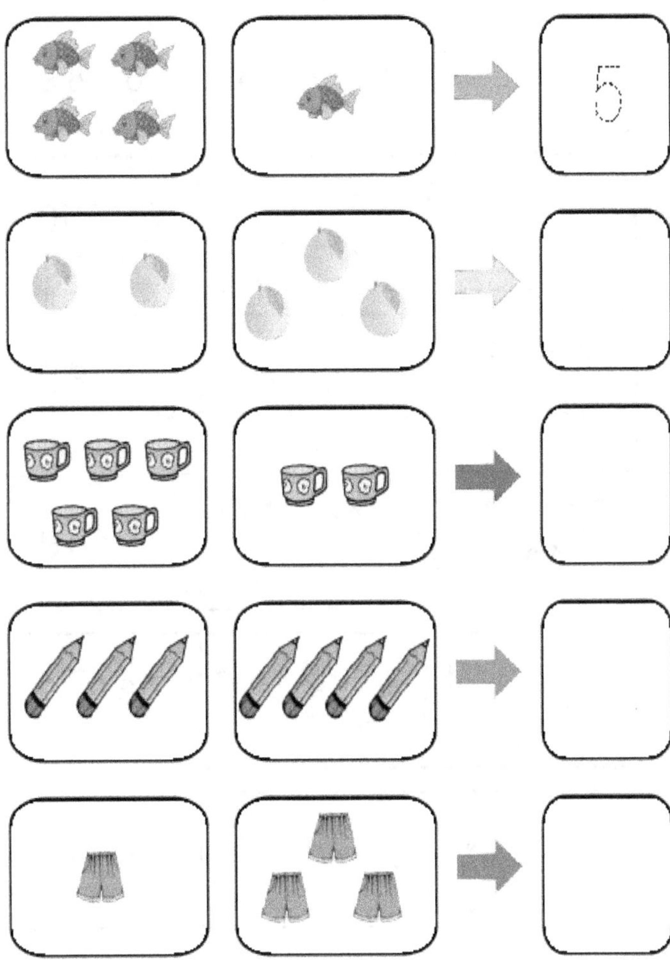

Name: ______________________

Counting Practice

Count and circle the right numbers.

	(6) 7 8 9
	7 8 9 10
	6 7 8 9
	6 7 8 9
	7 8 9 10
	6 7 8 9

Count and circle the correct numbers..

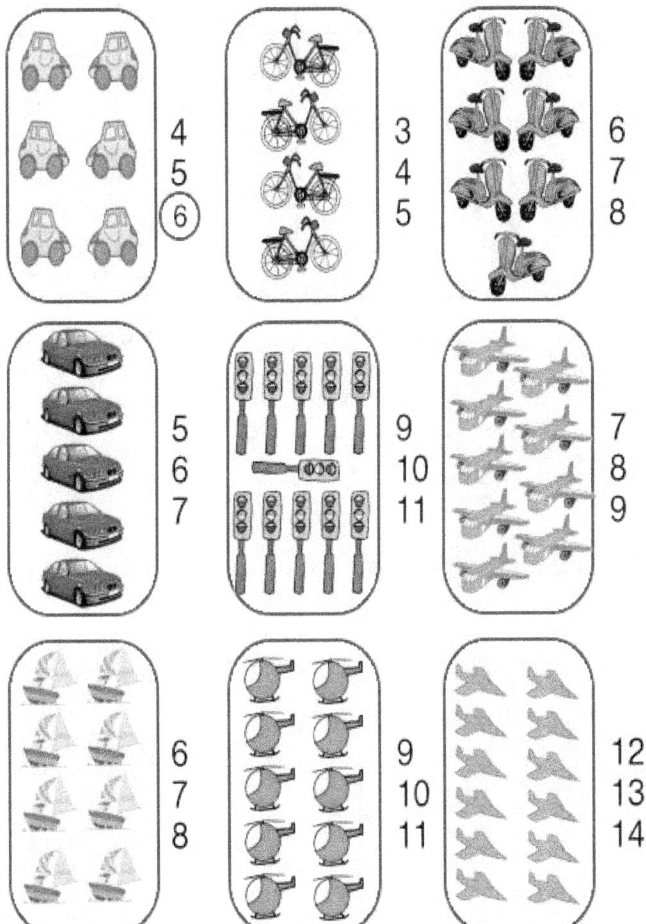

Counting practice up to 10.

Circle 2 parrots	Circle 5 cats
Circle 3 pigeons	Circle 6 rabbits
Circle 4 chickens	Circle 7 dogs

Counting Practice

Count and circle the right numbers.

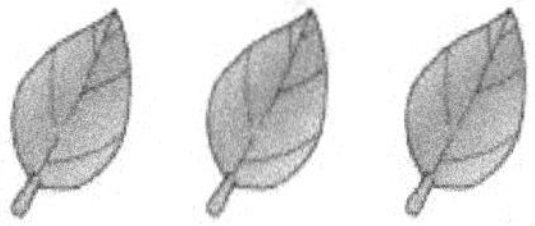

(3) 4 5 6	3 4 5 6
3 4 5 6	3 4 5 6
5 6 7 8	5 6 7 8

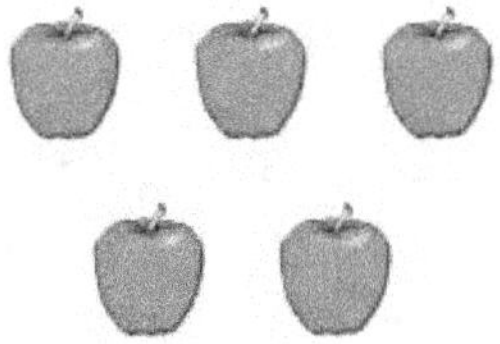

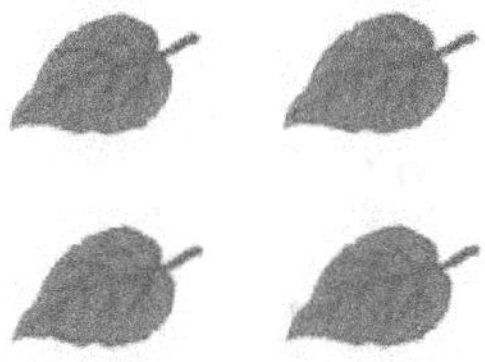

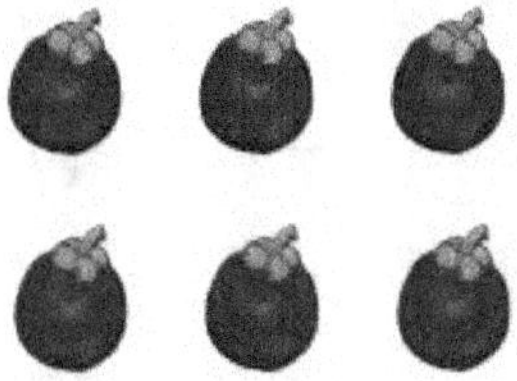

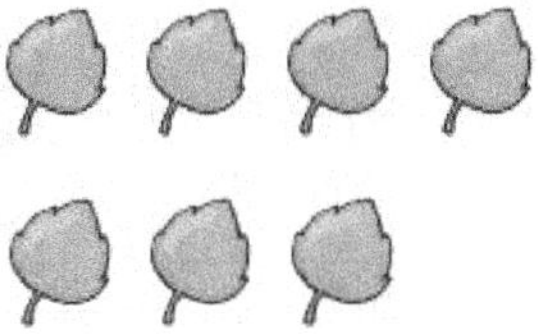

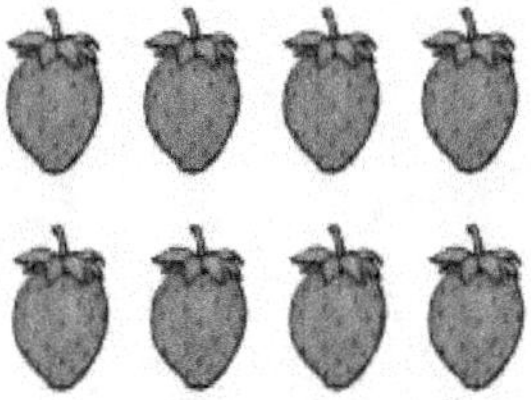

Basic Addition Worksheet with Sum to 5

Count and write the correct number in the box.

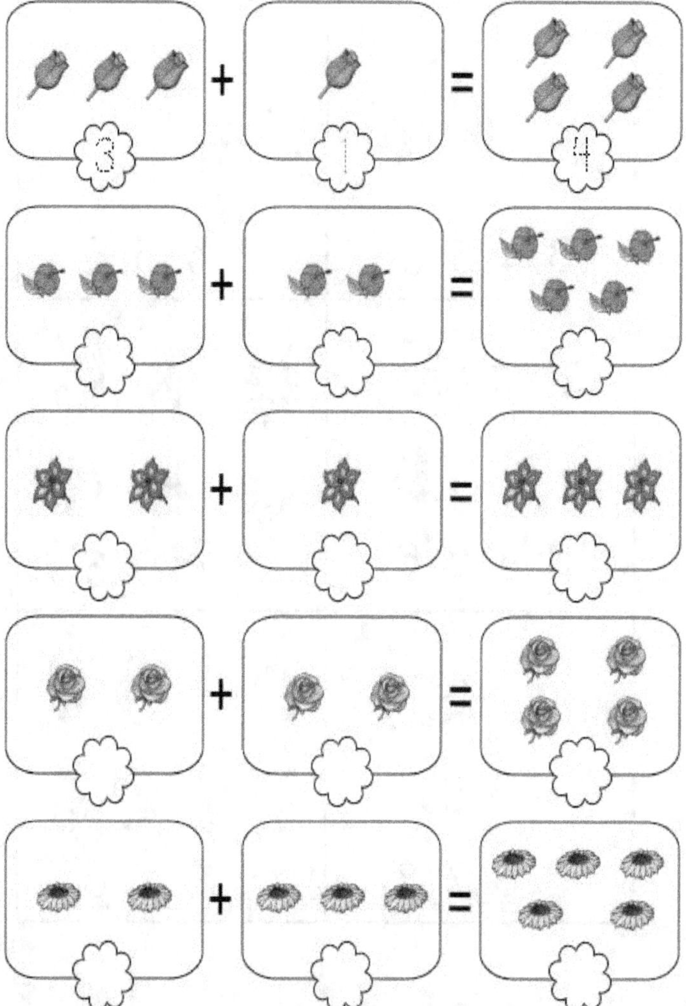

Basic Addition Worksheet with Sum to 10

Count and write the correct number in the box.

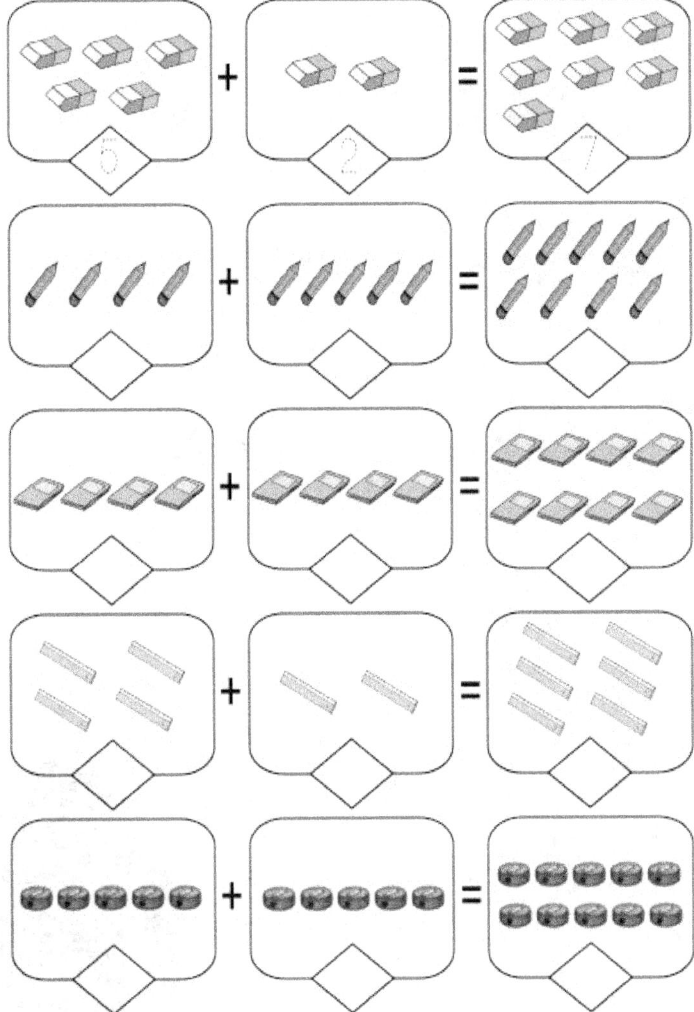

Pictures Addition With Sum to 10.

Count, sum and write the correct answer in the box.

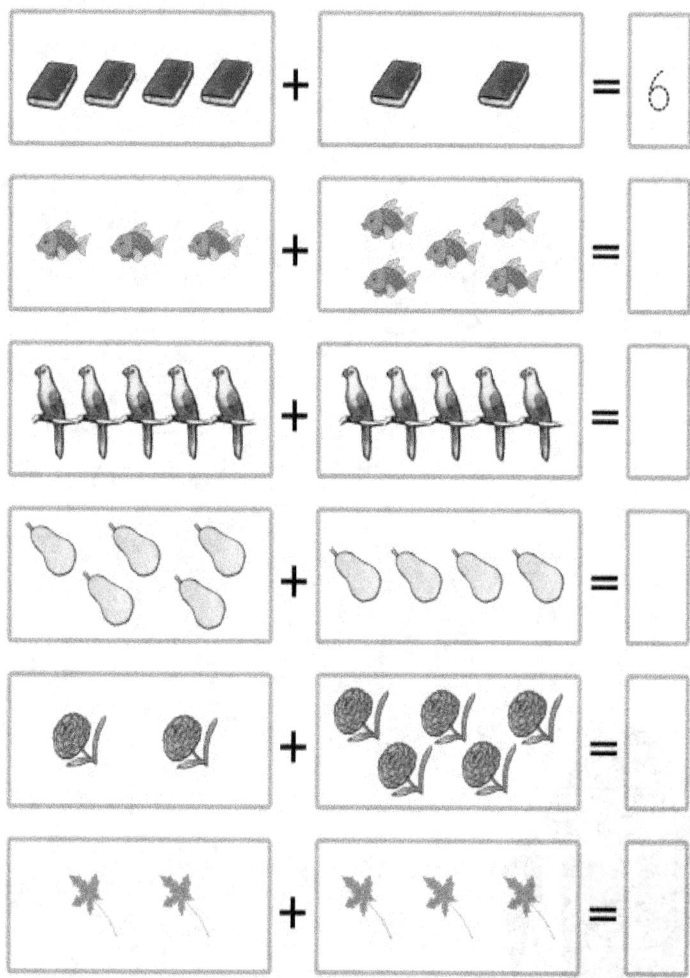

Pictures Addition With Sum to 10.

Count, sum and circle the correct number.

(3 shorts)	+ (4 shorts) =	7 8 9
(1 glasses)	+ (3 glasses) =	3 4 5
(4 shirts)	+ (2 shirts) =	6 7 8
(2 shoes)	+ (3 shoes) =	4 5 6
(6 caps)	+ (3 caps) =	7 8 9
(5 watches)	+ (3 watches) =	7 8 9

Pictures Addition With Sum to 10.

Count, sum and draw line to the correct number.

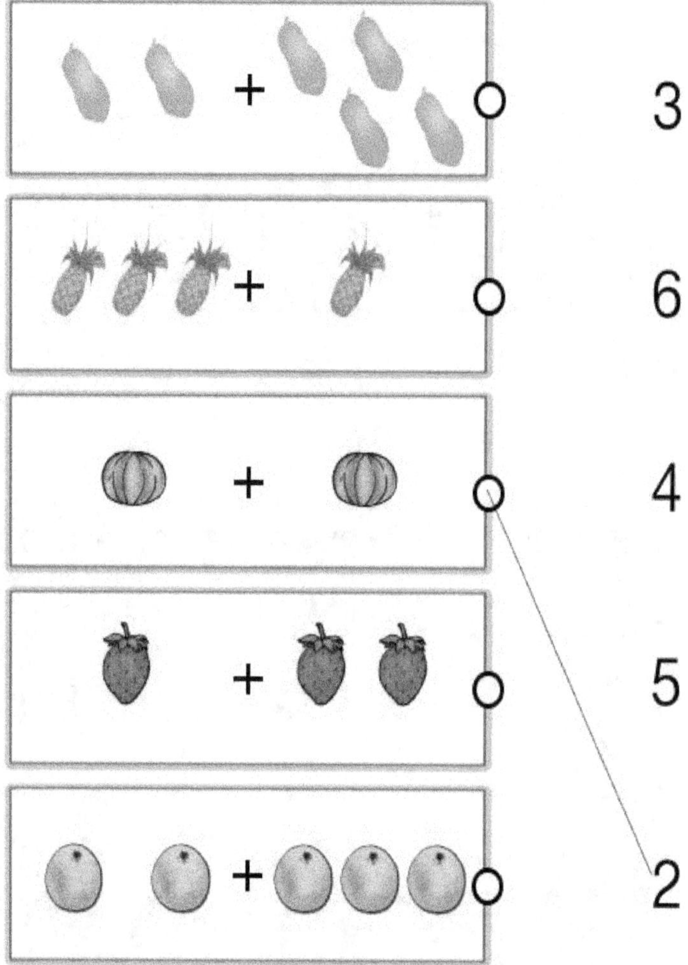

3

6

4

5

2

Addition with sums to 10

Sum and write the correct number in the box.

Addition with sums to 10

Sum and write the correct number in the box.

Subtracting up to 10

Subtract and write the correct number in the box.

(apples)	3 − 1 ···
(pears)	4 − 1 ···
(strawberries)	5 − 1 ···
(plums)	4 − 2 ···
(bananas)	3 − 2 ···

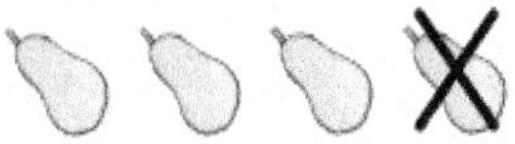

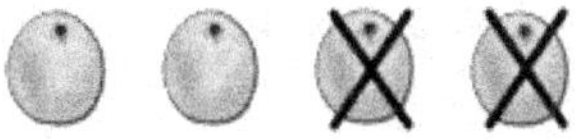

Subtracting up to 10

Subtract and write the correct number in the box.

Subtracting up to 10
Subtract and write the correct number in the box.

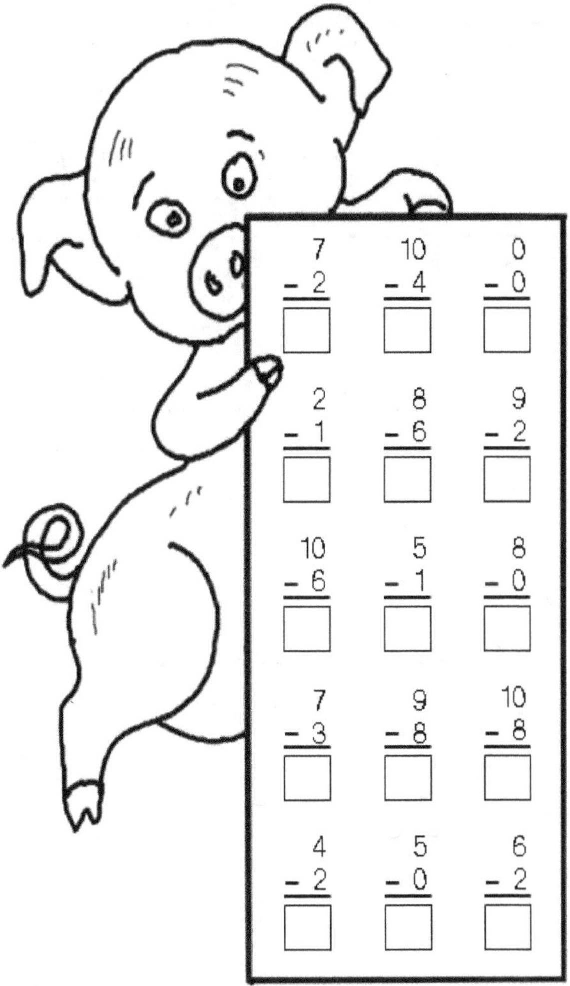

Trace the shapes below.

Counting shapes

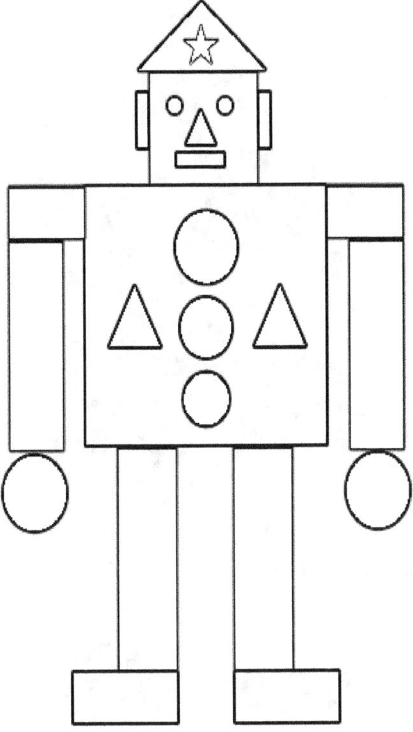

How many

Ordering Number 1 to 20

Reorder above number from the largest to the smallest number

Ordering Number 1 to 20

Reorder these numbers from the smallest to the largest number

Fill in the missing number.

Larger and smaller numbers.

Color the box with larger number.

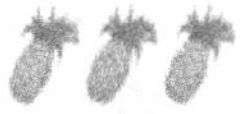	3
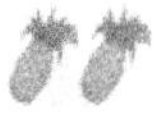	2

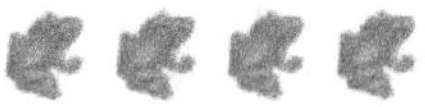	4
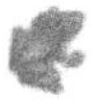	1

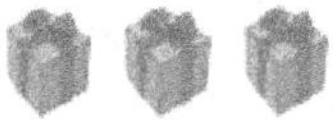	3
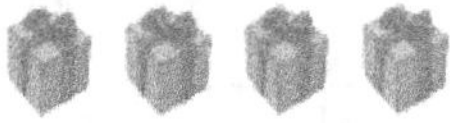	4

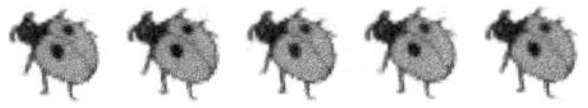	5
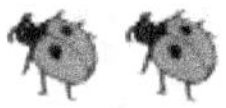	2

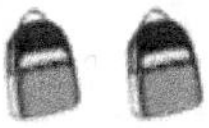	1
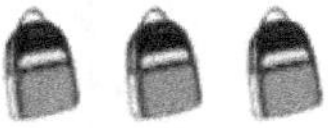	3

Larger and smaller numbers.

Color the box with larger number.

Larger and smaller numbers.

Color the box with smaller number.

Color and number.

Color 5 flowers	Color 8 balls
Color 6 tomatoes	Color 7 fishes

Color and number.

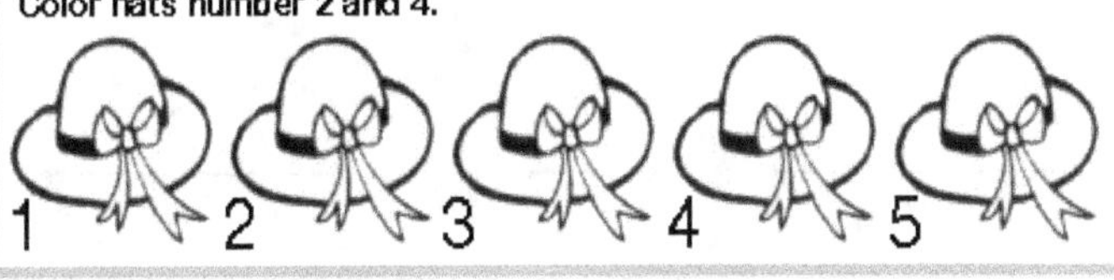

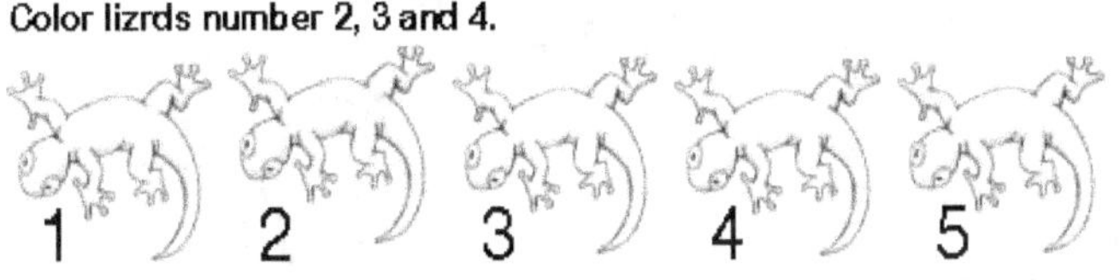

Color the number and the pictures.